If you've ever wanted to crawl in the closet with an OREO...

written by Martha Kate Down

2nd edition edited by Anne G. Stat⌐

Special thanks to Nabisco....
"OREO is a registered trademark of Nabisco Brands Company
and is used with permission."

And to **Anne Staton**...what would I do without you!

Books by MK

505 Anthony Dr.
Euless, TX 76039-2067
(817) 267-8563

www.mkdowney.com

Second Edition
ISBN 0-9742421-2-8
(previously ISBN 0-9650700-5-0 published 2000)

Printed and bound in the United States of America

Dedicated to Dennis,
my co-conspirator in this game called
"parenting".

And to our remarkable children,
David and Kate;
you are wonderful teachers...
just look at the great parents
you turned out!

Hi, I'm Martha Kate Downey, proud mother of two wonderful people, and wife to a caring, far-sighted, engineering-type husband. To say we have different parenting skills would be understating reality to the extreme. But, we both care intensely for our children and value our family, each other and our God. We have been enormously blessed.

That being said...There have been a few trials along the way (thirty years of marriage next year). One of the trials that turned into a blessing came to us in the form of Kate. We adopted Kate as a baby and discovered fairly early that we seemed to be living a different life-style than other parents with children her age. It was the beginning of a long search for a diagnosis and for help. This book includes some of those things I wish I had known when she was a little girl.

We have a very supportive family, but unfortunately they were as clueless as we were in providing answers to physical and behavioral issues that were "out of the norm". As an ex-social worker, it seemed natural for me to approach some of her care and education from that standpoint. Her "unusual" needs became a necessary focus while I tried to remain a stable parent for our son, who is 7 years older than Kate. It was not easy, but along the way we did find a few things that helped us.

Homeschooling was suggested to us as an option, and the suggestion proved to be a valuable one. It allowed us to use materials that best fit Kate's learning styles and, when needed, employ tutors who were adaptable and perceptive to Kate's unusual educational needs. I had the rewarding task of working with Kate for a prolonged period of time as she studied academics and practiced life skills. This gave me ample opportunity to study her language and behaviors first hand. In short, I came to know Kate very, very well.

Kate was originally diagnosed with Noonan Syndrome (NS). Some of the NS characteristics do fit Kate, but at the time of her diagnosis, the medical community had not yet clearly identified the realm of neurological functions that many individuals with Noonan's were displaying so I continued our search. She has a wide variety of diagnoses now, but autism (Asperger's Syndrome) seems to fit her best neurologically. For now, at age 17, that's where Kate chooses to hang her hat. Since Kate is NOT into the term "disabilities", she prefers to refer to her challenges as "differences". For me, those who are challenged with neurological or physical differences seem to add spice to the mixture of humanity. I think of our kids with special needs as each having his or her own *flavor*.

Our family still has much to learn, but what family doesn't? So for now, after 17 years with Kate and 22 years with David...here's a little that this Texas born and bred mother has learned and feels privileged to share.... MK (written in 1999)

Guess what my friend, Abby, teasingly said when I told her I was writing a book to share some of my more **positive** thoughts about parenting a child with special needs?

"Now here's a person living a **double life!**"
she said with a chuckle.

Okay, so I don't always remain in a positive
mind set. I often forget what I know... but
maybe writing this little book will help me
remember some of the things I've learned
over the past 27 years of parenting... and
maybe in the writing and remembering, I'll
feel a little better. Might even parent a tad
better!

So, as usual, thanks Abby, for everything.

MK

Have you ever wanted to lock yourself in your closet with a bagful of OREO cookies and a stack of cheap novels?

Then do it! Sometimes you just need a moment (or an hour, if you can get away with it) to glue yourself back together before re-entering the world of many demands. But first make sure your little darlings are safe and sound...otherwise, you're just sitting in a small space with bad books and ample calories worrying what they're into now!

Some of us have elevated
worrying

into an art form.

We've become professional *worriers.* We'll even worry for other peoples' kids if we think such anxiety is called for. Ever need someone else to worry about something for you? Call, I'm your gal; I'll do it for you! The only problem with worrying is that it's a thief of nighttime slumber and peace of mind. Don't let your own mind steal from you. Learn to dream those dreams that make you more creative, feel more positive and help you problem solve. Worry robs us of our mind's freedom to function in its best form.

Find a new form of art.

Speak

where you want your mind and heart
to follow.

You cannot always control things or people around you, but you may choose how your attitude will be directed. Dwell on how you want to think, feel and act, rather than the morose way you seem to be feeling at the time. If I talk about how bright my days with Kate are, I actually start feeling that way, too. It's a case of mind over matter.

Even if he is a biological child,

you're not **"guilty"** of anything !

One of the nicest things about adoption is that you don't have to assume genetic responsibility for any difficulties your child may have, but then you can't take credit for those wonderful traits that are inherited either. However, even as a biological parent, you had no control over which genes your little one selected *in utero*.

Give yourself a break!

You're not all-powerful!

Parenting is an ART FORM
... not a **science**

According to *Riverside Webster's II New College Dictionary*, art is:

1. "Human effort to imitate, supplement, alter, or counteract, the work of nature."

2. "A specific skill in adept performance, held to require the exercise of intuitive faculties that cannot be learned solely by study."

There are no definite answers to most questions regarding the raising of children...including those with special needs.

You have to gradually create, one stroke at a time, the type of parent each child needs. No two children will produce the same parents (since we know it is more a case of the child making the parent, rather than the parent making the child).

Let your child make you into

a beautiful *work of art!*

Some days it just gets down to a matter
of choosing whether to

laugh,

!*@^#&,
or
cry!

Face it,
your reaction won't change the facts...
just the way your stomach feels!

One word from experience...laughter will free your mind to think more positively and allow you to be a much more effective problem solver.

Getting respite **isn't** a *luxury* !

This one is
really,
really,
really,
really,
really,
really,
really,
really,
really,
really
hard for some of us to believe.

After all, we're supermoms and dads, *right?*

Get

HELP

when you can...

...even when you don't think you need it. It's sort of like building up a savings account... gives you a little cushion on really bad days.

Just because the help you found isn't
EXACTLY
what you had in mind...

Take it anyway,
it's better than nothing...
and you'll be **surprised** how often
it turns out to be better than
what you had in mind!

A
child
is
not
an alphabet.

Diagnoses come with letters and sometimes erroneous preconceptions. Unfortunately for some, words like "autism" or "mental retardation" are VERY frightening. So rather than explore the disorder further and take the help available from experts in that realm, many run away from help and deny a diagnosis. We may want to say, "Our child is NOT autistic," or "Our child is not mentally retarded!" But guess what?

A diagnosis does not a child make.

The letters assigned to a person do not create the person. No matter what alphabet is assigned to Kate, she is still just our Kate. Our embracing or avoiding a diagnosis does not change who she is at all, but can certainly change the amount of education or support we may get for her and for ourselves.

Through the years, Kate has had a real assortment of diagnoses. Like many of you, we've searched for just the "right" one. Each of the doctors seem to have their own alphabet to assign to her:

ADHD,
ADD,
NS,
TS,
WS,
AS,
OCD,
PDD-NOS and the list went on...

I thought that once we found the proper one, it would simply be a matter of learning about it and finding the "right" doctor to treat her.

Not necessarily!

In our case, one of Kate's original diagnoses was Noonan Syndrome (NS). At the time Kate was diagnosed, we were given some basic information about her physical conditions but very little about her behavioral or neurological functions. For years however, the behavioral and neurological aspects were the biggest issues we faced. So I spent those years searching for the "real" diagnosis.

Along the way we learned that even though a child has the diagnosis of a specific syndrome, she may not have all the symptoms. Also, while she may have some characteristics of another syndrome, she may not perfectly fit that diagnosis either.

Eventually, I came across Asperger Syndrome (AS), which is part of the autism spectrum. I immediately knew that we had found a good match for her behaviorally, so we began learning everything we could about Asperger's. But AS doesn't cover the physical characteristics that Noonan Syndrome covers. Does that mean that one of the diagnoses is wrong, or that the "real" diagnosis is still yet undetermined?
Not necessarily!

However, it does mean that chasing one specific diagnosis may not be as helpful as allowing the variety of diagnoses to act as road signs to resources for your child and your family.

Since Kate had symptoms of several different syndromes, we found ourselves searching for information in a variety of places. If The Association for Retarded Citizens (ARC) or the Autism Society or the Tourette Syndrome group had tips or services that would help us, we took them.

Some of the places we searched had information that was scary and required us to face our own fears about Kate and her future. Some required us to deal with our own pride and our personal expectations for ourselves, our own futures. But, after the initial shock from new diagnosis had worn off and we became more educated about that diagnosis, we began to realize that Kate had not changed, but rather our understanding of our roles as her parents. We were able to reidentify our skills for best helping her. We reflected that we had only been living with imagined futures, not real ones. The education we received didn't change Kate at all. Instead it affected our ability to help her and enhanced Kate's opportunity for self-growth.

Recycling

Save copies of documentation showing different diagnoses from different doctors...keep them all and use them in appropriate places to get the best services you can. I have a folder marked "Kate's diagnoses." Anytime she is applying for services from an agency or a school, we pull out and use the diagnosis that will enable her to qualify for the most benefits.

In short, having several diagnoses is really a pretty good thing! Kate's paperwork IS alphabet soup and that turned out to be mmmmm good!

Changing roles is harder than changing

Hats

!

Realize that having to quickly and frequently change parenting tasks is much harder than simply putting on a new hat or refocusing. It requires the ability to quickly draw on another set of skills, adjust your attitude, approach, and time frame.

Personally, I have always found it quite difficult to switch gears between:

writing,

teaching fractions,

unstopping the toilet!

I just don't have what it takes!

Some of the best work I've done as a stained glass artist occurred when I thought I didn't have the materials I needed. Necessity FORCED me to be creative and use what I had available in a new, exciting way. Creativity is a very important skill when parenting a child who comes in a different flavor.

Once I figured out that I didn't actually lack anything it became much easier to cope! I just needed to gather as much information as possible about Kate's syndromes, then brainstorm how to rearrange the skills and knowledge I had to a better advantage. The last and most important step was to trust that together we had all the "materials" necessary and could stand back and let creativity take over.

Parenting really IS an ART FORM!

Even though it sounds rather trite,
it really is

VERY IMPORTANT

to feel GOOD about yourself!

I think one of the hardest lessons in life is learning to accept positive things people say about us, including kudos about our parenting skills. We are most willing to accept blame, yet hesitant to acknowledge our successes.

That's not only hard on your digestive system, but even harder on your attitude! If you, or someone else acknowledges a positive trait about your parenting...

OWN it!
CELEBRATE it!
PRACTICE it!
And remember to say
"Thank you!"
(quite modestly, of course)

Fair ness

is a myth !

Letting go of some expectations and accepting that sometimes life just isn't "fair" helps me feel much less angry and frustrated... and leaves me feeling a whole lot less picked on!

(I know, easier said
than done.)

Some
bad stuff

is just going to happen...

it does to everyone!

Use those instances to teach your child how to cope with trials that come up in her own life, the same way you do.

The lesson here is NOT that your child is broken or damaged, but that bureaucratic systems, the public, or the schools may be unfair and create an even harder life for you and your child. These instances can make you or break you! Use them to show your child how to "pick herself up, dust herself off, and start all over again."

"Why?"

just doesn't work as a question.

Many kids with neurological differences are so driven by instinctive behavior, that they often have no conscious reason for their actions.

Unfortunately, many doctors, teachers, counselors (and parents, too) think that the child "**SHOULD**" have control over every thought and behavior. This doesn't mean that the child can't develop new control as he matures, but save your breath if you're trying to get motivational reasoning from a youngster about his instinctive behavior. You'll be more frustrated than the offender!

Your child might be able to tell you the events that happened prior to the behavior, and if you're a really good sleuth you might be able to figure out for yourself "why" the behavior occurred. But don't expect your insight to automatically alter the child's behavior. However, the discovery might give you clues for ways to "remodel" some of the more challenging behaviors.

When stuck,
don't just *SPIN YOUR WHEELS...*

Leave it awhile, take a fresh look later.

Sometimes it's not that you can't figure out the right approach to use...sometimes the child is just not developmentally ready to take on the task or new behavior. **No one's at fault**; it might just be time to take a break.

By the way, breaks can last anywhere from seconds...to years!

Understand that all you can do...
is what you CAN do!

Then be prepared to let some of the
responsibility pass into your children's hands.

In the final analysis, parents can't "live" or own the lives of their children. That means we must let them take responsibility for the people they become. Even those with many challenges must be allowed to have as much control as possible. Just like other children, parents have to allow them to learn from their mistakes...and revel in their successes!

When children make poor choices, don't put youself on trial, even if others try to force it upon you. In truth, you may only control yourself, which means

You're not the **"guilty"** defendant!

Just because our children choose to behave in a certain way does not make us guilty of their actions. If we've done the best we can to teach them the alternate method of choice (our choice, of course!), and they elect to follow another course of action, we are not responsible for that choice. That's what freedom is about. Children are entitled to the privilege of owning their own failures and successes. Otherwise, they are merely our puppets, and after a while you'll tire of playing puppeteer.

OR UNTANGLING THE STRINGS!

Scary times!

A few more words
from a mother struggling to let *go*....

Here's that issue of freedom again, one that I have found especially difficult to balance with Kate. When, how long, and to what extent do I impose my choices on her? You've probably noticed I still have feelings of push-pull in this area! I think that as she gets older, just setting a good example is perhaps the best guidance I can impose (oops, I mean "offer"!) And doing some self-talk, sort of like muttering out loud to myself as I make a personal decision, may help her understand how I make my own choices. Organizing all the information and making well thought-out decisions is definitely a difficult skill to learn. As children get older, decisions become more critical. One thing I've observed about Kate and her friends: the more they need guidance at the teenage stage in their lives, the less they want our help. Now is that normal or what!?!

Sometimes people and their lives get out of

Ba lanc e...

52

...just like the washing machine. The person or activity doesn't get attention 'til it completely breaks down. Get to know warning signs and sounds before the whole thing **bites the dust!**

Learn to figure out
whom
you're really mad at!

Fussing at the nearest person won't help correct the problem if the cause is someone, or something else.

Learn to correctly identify the irritant. This is a really important piece of detective work, well worth your time to solve!

p.s. You DO know that the only person you can really change is.......YOURSELF!

Don't borrow other people's anger...

Make sure that if you're angry at the school system, a neighbor, a doctor, or a friend, etc., it is because they (the person receiving your ill feelings) have actually done something to YOU... or maybe more importantly, your child! Don't take on someone else's anger just because that other person has a grievance. Someone else's experience may not be at all what your experience is. In short, we have plenty of grievances ourselves, without taking on someone else's.

p.s. Support groups often get into this trap! Be careful!

So, are you doing this just to bug me...

or can you really not help it?

For me, the hardest part about parenting a child with special needs is determining when not to let them "get away with" too much versus demanding things beyond their control. Identifying what really is within their ability to control is an incredibly hand-wrenching problem. Try going back to a list of characteristics that describes your child's diagnosis and see if the problem is included in those areas of "syndrome" behavior". The target problem or challenging behavior may be a characteristic that is just showing up in a new way. Be aware that your list of characteristics may not be complete. See if the behavior is following a trend seen in other areas of the child's behavior. Try some other techniques that may have worked in the past on similar behaviors to teach better habits. Still unsure??? Then...

Trust your gut
and
go for it!

Be aware that YOU, the parent, are the real authority! Doctors, counselors, administrators and teachers have far less instinctive or subconscious information than you have about your child. If you feel you're not getting the most appropriate services or information from "certified experts"...

Trust yourself!

But make sure you're not just living in that never, never world of denial or wishful thinking. This requires honest reactions and careful thought.

If you're really feeling

D

O

W

N

on yourself and your parenting...

Go ask someone who knows you well to list those things you ARE doing well. Make sure you tell them to refrain from mentioning the areas needing a little adjusting (even if you bring them up!!) Try asking your parents, your children, your friends, your cousin...maybe even your spouse.

You only have to do **today**...
today.

Trying to live in the future is probably the biggest depressor of all time, especially for those of us who are "*professional worriers.*" Don't let yourself be dragged into those thoughts of "what if." That doesn't mean not to plan ahead, but do it in a controlled, positive setting with some good resources. Then you feel better, not worse.

Growth comes in s p U rt s

Unfortunately, so does regression. Knowing that regression can be temporary and is not necessarily caused by some outside influence can take some of the sting out of it...kind of like baking soda on an insect bite; the bite's still there but it's tolerable.

Just because a skill is not there today,
doesn't mean it will never be there...

...but that hope can be a double-edged sword; one that could keep you from living with reality. Knowing how to hold the balance between

hope and **reality**

is
pretty
tricky.

As long as you have cards,

you haven't lost the game...

just perhaps the hand.

'Nuf said.

When you're faced with where you think

your child

SHOULD

be...

Remember that the absence or delay of traditional milestones may be especially traumatic and bring on depression for the parents...and maybe the kid, too.   Life's rituals or passages may catch you unaware. Focusing on the traditional timeline for driving a car or graduating from highschool can throw you into a downward spiral. Knowing that a milestone is potentially possible and preparing for it makes it pass much more easily.

I cope by remembering all the successes Kate has had, and we celebrate her hard won accomplishments.

It also helps if I identify some of the positive aspects of NOT experiencing the milestone (Not paying for more car insurance is a BIG one!)

Throw out that word

SHOULD

!

Learn to embrace what

IS

rather than what you WISH for
or
what you think **SHOULD** be.

SHOULD
just doesn't work for these kids;
they have their own **SHOULD** list...
unfortunately, we are not often
privy to it.

This is a necessary concept for relatives and teachers to know, too!

Throw out the saying...
"But we've always !!!"

(usually said with a bit of a whine)

Make it a tradition to be UNtraditional

No two Christmases at the Downey household have been exactly the same. Be willing to go with the flow. Plan events in such as way that they are fun, not mandatory. If your child's best time of the day is 7:00 p.m. do Christmas dinner then, rather than at a time when he is hungry and exhausted. By the next year, his best time may be 12 noon!

One year, your child may be most comfortable with only 2 or 3 people, so don't feel compelled to have 30 people, just because "we've always." A child's sense of security doesn't come from just "sameness", but rather from the knowledge that events are not out of his comfort zone or your control. One year on Christmas Day, there were just the four of us. We decided to go out and have a fancy meal that someone else cooked. Great time! But I wouldn't want to do it every year!

Your child has her own calendar.

Throw yours away!

Be aware that just because your child didn't act like a typical 13-year-old at age 13...doesn't mean that she never will have 13-year-old behavior. Most of the growing-up phases seem to come, just not necessarily at traditional times. And they won't necessarily be over in "typical" lengths of time, either. You may have a 17-year-old daughter with a thirteen-year-old attitude!

But remember...if at all possible...this is just a stage! Say it to yourself 88 times per day: *"This is just a stage, this is just a stage, this is just a stage, this is just a stage, this is just a stage, this is just a stage, this is just a stage, this is just a stage, this is just a stage, this...*

It's not your imagination...

every day

IS

a whole

new

DAY!

Our kids don't function the same way each day. What they knew yesterday may not be there today... but, the skill or knowledge might be back tomorrow.

Make it your **1st**,
most important job to be in charge of
fun!

Think of the good things that come out of fun. You might discover new people, new ideas. You'll have more laughter. Laughter, like an internal massage, loosens you up, helps get rid of some of the **SHOULD**s. I know it gets me into lots of trouble on the Internet! I've been chastised, ignored, and nearly banned from online support groups for creating too much fun, but I still think providing respite from tension is sometimes the best support I can give. I have limited wisdom to offer, but fun I can usually dream up!   That's a real life saver when dealing with these pretty "un-fun" kinds of issues. I don't mean ignore them, and you have to find the right time for entertainment, but make sure everyday has something **fun** in it! (EVEN if you're spending everyday in the hospital as a caregiver or a patient... ESPECIALLY if you're spending every day in the hospital !)

Examples of *fun* please...

* Watching a favorite show

* having a long heart-to-heart talk
   with a goldfish ???

* *playing a game*

* even sitting in the closet...

   (with the proper supplies, of course!)

p.s. It doesn't count if you're feeling guilty while you're
having your fun!

Send yourself to your room

when necessary.

When your child is really out of control, you'll often realize there's no way you could get him to go to his room for a cooling off period. So. if the child is not in imminent danger (from someone or something other than you!) go to your own room (but don't close the door). By focusing on **yourself** and **your** needs in the new location you won't feel compelled to continue the turmoil.

Take a break, regroup, wash your face, call a friend on the phone, etc...Your child will likely follow you and see how you regroup and cool off...'course you may be forced to share your stash of OREOs if that is what you had in mind!

me...........and Kate

WORK FROM MORE THAN ONE ANGLE.

SOLVE THE PROBLEM BY LOOKING AT IT...

with a new perspective.

When you're completely and hopelessly
frustrated with your kid...

Focus on **yourself**. Let's face it, while we think we're pretty powerful, we're really not! (Sorry to deliver that piece of unwelcome news to all those authors and authorities who are writing about how to get your kid to be what you want her to be.) The only person you can really control and change is yourself! See if your own reactions are just contributing to the problem and rethink the necessity of the "wished for" behavior of your child. It may be that you've slipped, unwittingly, back into those binding (and unrealistic!) expectations of "**SHOULDS**" or the mythical fantasyland of "FAIR".

Just because something worked with one kid doesn't necessarily mean it will work with another.

Often, common methods of dealing with behavioral issues won't work with your flavorful child. You may need to experiment with new or different ones. Instead of cause/effect type stuff, try repetition: practice a skill over and over...like taking the laundry upstairs and putting it in the drawers 5 times.

Another little tidbit of information I've gleaned over the years...a teacher or instructor who was wonderful with one of your children, WON'T necessarily be wonderful with your next child.

Don't make big decisions during acts of

passion

(especially if you're feeling passionately angry!)

Passion has a way of taking everything out of proportion!

Passion blocks the ability to recognize and evaluate necessary information to make a reasonable decision.

Don't assume
that just because they say
or repeat something...
they know what they said!

These kids have lots of communication glitches. Make sure you use all the tools you can for communication...

Sign language,
pictures,
observation,
contextual clues (noticing things not said),
role play,
self-talk.

Less **talk** -

more ***action***

Some kids learn much more from
direct intervention
than from
lots of talking!

Demonstrate the behavior
you want.

(Or gently, silently take them by the hand and go
through the desired process WITH them.)

When worse comes to worse

RUN AWAY...

... TOGETHER

Sometimes everyone needs to run away. Just throw up your hands and walk away, with your child's hand in yours. Go do something completely different, in a new space and with a different emotion and frame of mind. Try lying in the backyard and looking at the clouds, making a peanut butter sandwich and walking down the street....

Speaking of *running away...*

It's okay to occasionally take a "mental health" day...blowing off the whole day, not accomplishing a thing...making that the whole purpose of the day. Kate and I call them "*play days*". We try to do at least one each season, to celebrate the season.

Learn how to

celebrate!

celebrate!

Kate has a great sense of *celebration*. It sort of goes along with her famous saying, "The worst disability is a bad attitude." She's so right! People with poor attitudes have a very limited sense of appreciation. A sense of *celebration* creates an ability to marvel at all the opportunities and blessings life has to offer.

celebrate!

Consider
" the hassle factor."

Is a school or an agency delivering enough beneficial service to warrant all the hassle of receiving the service? If not, go down another avenue or do it yourself.

Count the costs both ways.

Example: Kate hated physical therapy at the hospital, but loved dance classes. We were lucky to find instructors that could take goals we had for her and adapt them to a dance form. This was considerably more fun for us all and a whale of a lot cheaper!

(Especially, since what we deemed as "essential", our insurance company called "optional".)

Many children get into trouble when they are
bored...

If your children are getting into even more trouble than usual, it may simply be a problem of lack of focus, attention or direction. They may need a hobby, a new book, a friend to play a game, or a mind-consuming project to think about.

Risk being W*EIr*D

Sometimes the very thing that seems wrong or backward...
may be just the RIGHT thing for your flavorful child.

Usually you can't hide your

CHILD

with differences.

You just think you have. Parents of children with differences, disabilities or handicaps may often think no one notices that their child is a little "off the beaten track." Often others do notice, but don't know how to react to your child or how to get information about the disability. We've learned that it is better to willingly and openly talk about the syndrome or behaviors. The public then sees the differences through our educated, accepting eyes rather than through their own fearful, confused, inexperienced eyes.

Some days the planets just won't hold
a plumb line...

O
  O
  O

O
  O
O
O
O
O

Be aware that other things are going to color your parenting (for the better or for the worse). Sometimes you just feel rotten in general, but it has nothing to do with your kid.

Parenting doesn't have to match
to be consistent.

One of the best things about the two-parent system is the fact that you can share values but not necessarily use the same parenting methods. (Although the extent of difference depends on the limitations of the child.) Teaching children with more than one approach is sometimes very effective. You don't have to copy your spouse's parenting style to be consistent if you maintain the same expectations and values.

If it won't make any difference to the world
(or even to you) in five years...
it's really not that important.
Let it go!

Many of the things we parents get so worked up about simply aren't worth the effort we expend or the anxiety we cause ourselves or our children. If the issue won't make any difference in a few years...

let

it

go.

Planning to live **forever**???????????????????

120

"Unless you want to fold **every towel** in your household for the **rest of eternity**...learn to live with someone else's folding technique."

Thank you, Mother, for that wise bit of information!

(I guess that applies to other things, too, huh?)

When a
NEGATIVE turns into a **POSITIVE**...

...IT IS SUCH AN EXCITING THING!

Kate's perseveration (concentrating on one thing and one thing only) is wonderfully helpful when she is given a challenge requiring vigilance, and her loud voice is quite handy when getting the attention of a roomful of kids. Recognizing the positive sides of challenging behaviors may take practice on your part as a parent, but once you get the hang of it your child will

shine !

As a parent

of a *flavorful* child,

be prepared for a *roller coaster ride*.

It is exciting, yet scary, when children begin to step out on their own. Many times you'll think how much easier it would be to do something for them rather than watch them struggle to complete the task themselves. However, to quote a very wise woman, *"You don't help people by doing things for them that they could do for themselves. That's how you cripple them."* So rather than stopping them from developing as fully as possible you have to learn to

hang on, and enjoy the thrill!

When you know a big change or challenge is
coming your way...

...try to place on the back burner some of the less critical areas of your life. Let go of some extraneous activities 'til you have adjusted to the new challenge or the crisis has passed. Otherwise, the whole house of cards will fall in.

Trust me, I KNOW about this one!

A very novel thought:

It's okay for parents to have special needs, too! Kate was 15 before that occurred to me. Around here, Kate is a very important person. We try to help her in as many ways as we can. But I finally realized one day, when I was completely frustrated, that it was okay if I had some of my more exceptional needs met as well. I did not intend to be a martyr, but every time I put my desires or needs before Kate's or David's, I usually carried my close friend "guilt" along beside me.

I knew in my mind that Kate was PART of the family, not ALL of the family and that she was **no more** important, or special than any other member. That concept had always been with me, but for some reason I had never fully applied the theory because I failed to consider myself part of the equation.

One day it struck me that it was acceptable to demand that Kate put my needs before hers. While that concept is still harder for me to grasp than for Kate to practice, she was most willing to accept this occasional shift. Parents become so accustomed to taking care of children and sacrificing for them that they forget to let their children learn to sacrifice and be the caregivers. Kate welcomed the idea and joyfully became the giver of compassionate care. I discovered that she needed to provide service for others not only to fully develop, but to build confidence and assurance that she is truly needed! (I'm slowly learning it is okay to be a *MOM* with "special needs"!)

Parents' self-esteem
affects their parenting.

My disposition directly affects the dispositions of everyone else in our household. So, how do we keep ourselves moving in a positive direction through all the turmoil that surrounds us? Through the years I've had the opportunity to sample a variety of methods to keep me going...or GET me going again! I've found these helpful: praying, counseling, venting, talking where you want to be, journaling, doing art projects, gardening, reading, calling my cousin, making a list of accomplishments, getting organized (you'll be surprised how effective that is)! Learn to identify those things that make you feel better and employ them when they're needed, rather than waiting 'til they occur by happenstance.

Kate is part of my life...

not ALL of my life!

132

While parenting is the most time consuming, mind consuming activity I have ever experienced, I still have parts of my life that are not shared with my children. I value those. It helps my state of mind and body to pursue other interests. These personal activities are important for me to develop and nurture. When you are having especially difficult times with a child (surgery, severe illness, behavioral issues that you can't seem to solve), these other areas may provide respite for your mind. My alternate realms offer comfort, positive feedback and relief from worry. Stepping out and away from turmoil often yields the ability to return rejuvenated and with a different outlook. I've found this to be a great problem solving technique. Your children need this sort of role modeling to develop themselves fully as well.

Make
some
friends...

...with parents of other flavorful kids. It's so nice to have safe places to go where you won't be judged and your child will be accepted. Friends whose children have never met these kinds of challenges will sometimes have a hard time relating to your life.

We have received another big bonus as the parents of a flavorful child. It came to us as a result of Kate's magnetism. It's as if she is a magnet for wonderfully kind, creative and generous souls. So many of these people would never have crossed our paths had she not drawn them to us.

Are there some years that are just HARD?

Yes, but generally they are ones with much potential for growth. When you have one of these difficult years, remember to spend extra time with those people who provide emotional support. Schedule in fun, take frequent breaks and have more play days. Make sure you pay careful attention to things such as eating and sleeping well. It's like having chicken soup when you have a cold.

These hard years provide ample opportunity to learn the lessons our children can teach. They are GREAT years to learn compassion, creativity, patience and humility. We rarely learn important life lessons in the EASY years!

What in the world do I have to offer?

When you wonder if you have what it takes to parent a child...think of the positives in your child's life. Somehow these positives were encouraged. For example, Kate is now 21 and she's still around, so I must have a fair degree of **patience**. We haven't given her back (adoption is a forever kind of thing in our household), so I must have a pretty good amount of **stick-to-it-tiveness**. We've never had to visit her in jail, so she must have gotten SOME **values** from SOMEWHERE! She has wonderful friends who are terrific people, so she must be somewhat socially acceptable!

Last, but not necessarily least, Kate has acquired some sort of education...eccentric though it may be. Homeschooling a student with autism is not only challenging, it's exciting!!! Thus, I must be **brave** enough to handle the roller coaster ride!

Here is the important issue: your skills as a parent won't be identical to my skills. You are unique, and your child is unique. It is essential, however, that any person's skills are recognized and appreciated. Think of parenting skills as tools in a large tool box. As your experience increases, so do the number of tools you have. Each of us grab for different tools; some of us are working on wood and some metal. We each add tools specifically designed to facilitate our own individual project.

So... when the times get rough, keep your toolbox handy and your closet stocked with all those things that give you comfort and get you back into top form. (Note to MK: Put this book in the closet next to the cheap novels.) Remember... somewhere there's another parent sitting in a closet and sharing an OREO with you, celebrating, of course, what we all are...

GREAT PARENTS !

Why OREO ??

No one knows exactly when the OREO cookie was first used as an international symbol of comfort. However, its use in this book was inspired by The Noonan Syndrome Support Group (TNSSG). For several years their online support network, as well as others, has shared a "cyber-OREO" with friends needing comfort.

The world-wide web has connected families of children with special needs from far and wide, enabling parents of children with even the most rare disorders to support one another. Because of the distance, however, it is often not possible to take a casserole to their homes, or offer a comforting hug during times of distress. The OREO has come to symbolize that casserole, that touch of warmth, extended between families.

Our thanks to Nabisco for permission to use the OREO trademark in this book. OREO has special meaning to many families around the world.

Books by MK

505 Anthony Drive
Euless, TX 76039
(817) 267-8563
mk@mkdowney.com

www.mkdowney.com

****

Books by this author:
If you've ever wanted to crawl in the closet with an OREO...
TAP DANCING in th night
The People in a Girl's Life
What Do I Do About Hitting?!